Key Facts™ on Kuwait

~Essential Information on Kuwait~

By Patrick W. Nee

The Internationalist®

www.internationalist.com

The Internationalist®

International Business, Investment, and Travel

Published by:

The Internationalist Publishing Company

96 Walter Street/ Suite 200

Boston, MA 02131, USA

Tel: 617-354-7722

www.internationalist.com

PN@internationalist.com

Copyright © 2014 by PWN

The Internationalist is a Registered Trademark. "Key Facts" and "The Internationalist Business Guides" are Trademarks of The Internationalist Publishing Company.

All Rights are reserved under International, Pan-American, and Pan-Asian Conventions. No part of this book may be reproduced in any form without the written permission of the publisher. All rights vigorously enforced

Table Of Contents

Chapter 1: Background
Chapter 2: Geography
Chapter 3: People and Society
Chapter 4: Government and Key Leaders
Chapter 5: Economy
Chapter 6: Energy
Chapter 7: Communications
Chapter 8: Transportation
Chapter 9: Military
Chapter 10: Transnational Issues
Map of Kuwait

Chapter 1: Background

Britain oversaw foreign relations and defense for the ruling Kuwaiti AL-SABAH dynasty from 1899 until independence in 1961. Kuwait was attacked and overrun by Iraq on 2 August 1990. Following several weeks of aerial bombardment, a US-led, UN coalition began a ground assault on 23 February 1991 that liberated Kuwait in four days. Kuwait spent more than $5 billion to repair oil infrastructure damaged during 1990-91. The AL-SABAH family has ruled since returning to power in 1991 and reestablished an elected legislature that in recent years has become increasingly assertive. The country witnessed the historic election in May 2009 of four women to its National Assembly. Amid the 2010-11 uprisings and protests across the Arab world, stateless Arabs, known as bidoon, staged small protests in February and March 2011 demanding citizenship, jobs, and other benefits available to Kuwaiti nationals. Youth activist groups - supported by opposition legislators and the prime minister's rivals within the ruling family - rallied repeatedly in 2011 for an end to corruption and the ouster of the prime minister and his cabinet. Opposition legislators forced the prime minister to resign in late 2011. In October-December 2012, Kuwait witnessed unprecedented protests in response to the Amir's changes to the electoral law by decree reducing the number of votes per person from four to one. The opposition, led by a coalition of Sunni Islamists, tribalists, some liberals, and myriad youth groups, boycotted the December 2012 legislative election, resulting in a historic number of Shia candidates winning seats. Since 2006, the Amir has dissolved the National Assembly on five occasions (the Constitutional Court annulled the Assembly once in June 2012) and reshuffled the cabinet 12 times, usually citing political stagnation and gridlock between the legislature and the government.

Chapter 2: Geography

Location:
　　Middle East, bordering the Persian Gulf, between Iraq and Saudi Arabia

Geographic coordinates:
　　29 30 N, 45 45 E

Map references:
　　Middle East

Area:
　　total: 17,818 sq km
　　country comparison to the world: 158
　　land: 17,818 sq km
　　water: 0 sq km

Area - comparative:
　　slightly smaller than New Jersey

Land boundaries:
　　total: 462 km
　　border countries: Iraq 240 km, Saudi Arabia 222 km

Coastline:
　　499 km

Maritime claims:
　　territorial sea: 12 nm

Climate:
　　dry desert; intensely hot summers; short, cool winters

Terrain:
　　flat to slightly undulating desert plain

Elevation extremes:
　　lowest point: Persian Gulf 0 m
　　highest point: unnamed elevation 306 m

Natural resources:
　　petroleum, fish, shrimp, natural gas

Land use:
> arable land: 0.62%
> permanent crops: 0.28%
> other: 99.1% (2011)

Irrigated land:
> 86 sq km (2007)

Total renewable water resources:
> 0.02 cu km (2011)

Freshwater withdrawal (domestic/industrial/agricultural):
> total: 0.91 cu km/yr (47%/2%/51%)
> per capita: 441.2 cu m/yr (2005)

Natural hazards:
> sudden cloudbursts are common from October to April and bring heavy rain, which can damage roads and houses; sandstorms and dust storms occur throughout the year but are most common between March and August

Environment - current issues:
> limited natural freshwater resources; some of world's largest and most sophisticated desalination facilities provide much of the water; air and water pollution; desertification

Environment - international agreements:
> party to: Biodiversity, Climate Change, Climate Change-Kyoto Protocol, Desertification, Endangered Species, Environmental Modification, Hazardous Wastes, Law of the Sea, Ozone Layer Protection
> signed, but not ratified: Marine Dumping

Geography - note:
> strategic location at head of Persian Gulf

Chapter 3: People and Society

Nationality:

    noun: Kuwaiti(s)

    adjective: Kuwaiti

Ethnic groups:

    Kuwaiti 45%, other Arab 35%, South Asian 9%, Iranian 4%, other 7%

Languages:

    Arabic (official), English widely spoken

Religions:

    Muslim (official) 85% (Sunni 70%, Shia 30%), other (includes Christian, Hindu, Parsi) 15%

Population:

    2,695,316 (July 2013 est.)

    country comparison to the world: 140

    note: includes 1,291,354 non-nationals

Age structure:

    0-14 years: 25.6% (male 358,415/female 330,467)

    15-24 years: 15.4% (male 228,147/female 187,035)

    25-54 years: 52.3% (male 896,693/female 514,196)

    55-64 years: 4.5% (male 70,863/female 51,660)

    65 years and over: 2.1% (male 27,995/female 29,845) (2013 est.)

Median age:

    total: 28.8 years

    male: 30 years

    female: 26.6 years (2013 est.)

Population growth rate:

    1.79%

    country comparison to the world: 68

    note: this rate reflects a return to pre-Gulf crisis immigration of expatriates (2013 est.)

Birth rate:

20.61 births/1,000 population (2013 est.)

country comparison to the world: 82

Death rate:

2.14 deaths/1,000 population (2013 est.)

country comparison to the world: 222

Net migration rate:

-0.59 migrant(s)/1,000 population (2013 est.)

country comparison to the world: 136

Urbanization:

urban population: 98.3% of total population (2011)

rate of urbanization: 2.42% annual rate of change (2010-15 est.)

Major urban areas - population:

KUWAIT (capital) 2.23 million (2009)

Sex ratio:

at birth: 1.05 male(s)/female

0-14 years: 1.09 male(s)/female

15-24 years: 1.22 male(s)/female

25-54 years: 1.75 male(s)/female

55-64 years: 1.4 male(s)/female

65 years and over: 0.96 male(s)/female

total population: 1.43 male(s)/female (2013 est.)

Maternal mortality rate:

14 deaths/100,000 live births (2010)

country comparison to the world: 145

Infant mortality rate:

total: 7.68 deaths/1,000 live births

country comparison to the world: 159

male: 7.41 deaths/1,000 live births

female: 7.95 deaths/1,000 live births (2013 est.)

Life expectancy at birth:

total population: 77.46 years

country comparison to the world: 66

male: 76.24 years

female: 78.75 years (2013 est.)

Total fertility rate:

2.56 children born/woman (2013 est.)

country comparison to the world: 79

Contraceptive prevalence rate:

52% (1999)

Health expenditures:

2.6% of GDP (2010)

country comparison to the world: 185

Physicians density:

1.79 physicians/1,000 population (2009)

Hospital bed density:

2 beds/1,000 population (2009)

Drinking water source:

improved:

urban: 99% of population

rural: 99% of population

total: 99% of population

unimproved:

urban: 1% of population

rural: 1% of population

total: 1% of population (2010 est.)

Sanitation facility access:

improved:

urban: 100% of population

rural: 100% of population

total: 100% of population (2010 est.)

HIV/AIDS - adult prevalence rate:

0.1% (2001 est.)

country comparison to the world: 143
HIV/AIDS - people living with HIV/AIDS:
NA (2007 est.)
HIV/AIDS - deaths:
NA
Obesity - adult prevalence rate:
42% (2008)
country comparison to the world: 10
Children under the age of 5 years underweight:
1.7% (2009)
country comparison to the world: 122
Education expenditures:
3.8% of GDP (2006)
country comparison to the world: 120
Literacy:
definition: age 15 and over can read and write
total population: 93.3%
male: 94.4%
female: 91% (2005 census)
School life expectancy (primary to tertiary education):
total: 14 years
male: 13 years
female: 15 years (2004)
Unemployment, youth ages 15-24:
total: 11.3%
country comparison to the world: 102
male: 11.8%
female: 10% (2005)

Chapter 4: Government and Key Leaders

Country name:

    conventional long form: State of Kuwait

    conventional short form: Kuwait

    local long form: Dawlat al Kuwayt

    local short form: Al Kuwayt

Government type:

    constitutional emirate

Capital:

    name: Kuwait City

    geographic coordinates: 29 22 N, 47 58 E

    time difference: UTC+3 (8 hours ahead of Washington, DC during Standard Time)

Administrative divisions:

    6 governorates (muhafazat, singular - muhafazah); Al Ahmadi, Al 'Asimah, Al Farwaniyah, Al Jahra', Hawalli, Mubarak al Kabir

Independence:

    19 June 1961 (from the UK)

National holiday:

    National Day, 25 February (1950)

Constitution:

    approved and promulgated 11 November 1962

Legal system:

    mixed legal system consisting of English common law, French civil law, and Islamic religious law

International law organization participation:

    has not submitted an ICJ jurisdiction declaration; non-party state to the ICCt

Suffrage:

    21 years of age; universal; note - males in the military or police are by law not allowed to vote; all voters must have been citizens for 20 years

Executive branch:

chief of state: Amir SABAH al-Ahmad al-Jabir al-Sabah (since 29 January 2006); Crown Prince NAWAF al-Ahmad al-Jabir al-Sabah (born 25 June 1937)

head of government: Prime Minister JABIR AL-MUBARAK al-Hamad al-Sabah (since 30 November 2011); First Deputy Prime Minister AHMAD al-Hamud al-Jabir al-Sabah; Deputy Prime Ministers AHMAD AL-KHALID al-Hamad al-Sabah, SABAH AL-KHALID al-Hamad al-Sabah, Mustafa al-Jassim al-SHAMALI

cabinet: Council of Ministers appointed by the prime minister and approved by the amir; new cabinet formed in February 2012

elections: none; the amir is hereditary; the amir appoints the prime minister and deputy prime ministers

Legislative branch:

unicameral National Assembly or Majlis al-Umma (65 seats - 50 members elected by popular vote plus 16 cabinet ministers, one of whom is also an elected MP, appointed by the prime minister as ex officio voting members; elected members serve four-year terms); note - the National Assembly was dissolved on 7 October 2012

elections: last held 27 July 2013 (next to be held in July 2017)

election results: percent of vote - NA; seats won – tribal and liberal groups 27, Shiite 8, Sunni 7, other 8

Judicial branch:

highest court(s): Constitutional Court (five judges); Supreme Court or Court of Cassation (organized into several circuits, each with five judges)

judge selection and term of office: all Kuwaiti judges appointed by the Amir upon recommendation of the Supreme Judicial Council, a consultative body comprised of Kuwaiti judges and Ministry of Justice officials

subordinate courts: High Court of Appeal; Court of First Instance; Summary Court

Political parties and leaders:

none; while the formation of political parties is not permitted, they are not forbidden by law

Political pressure groups and leaders:

other: Islamists; merchants; political groups; secular liberals and pro-governmental deputies; Shia activists; tribal groups

International organization participation:
ABEDA, AfDB (nonregional member), AFESD, AMF, BDEAC, CAEU, CD, FAO, G-77, GCC, IAEA, IBRD, ICAO, ICC (national committees), ICRM, IDA, IDB, IFAD, IFC, IFRCS, IHO, ILO, IMF, IMO, IMSO, Interpol, IOC, IPU, ISO, ITSO, ITU, ITUC (NGOs), LAS, MIGA, NAM, OAPEC, OIC, OPCW, OPEC, Paris Club (associate), PCA, UN, UNCTAD, UNESCO, UNIDO, UNRWA, UNWTO, UPU, WCO, WFTU (NGOs), WHO, WIPO, WMO, WTO

Diplomatic representation in the US:
chief of mission: Ambassador SALIM al-Abdallah al-Jabir al-Sabah
chancery: 2940 Tilden Street NW, Washington, DC 20008
telephone: [1] (202) 966-0702
FAX: [1] (202) 364-2868
consulate(s) general: Los Angeles

Diplomatic representation from the US:
chief of mission: Ambassador Matthew H. TUELLER
embassy: Bayan 36302, Block 13, Al-Masjed Al-Aqsa Street (near the Bayan palace), Kuwait City
mailing address: P. O. Box 77 Safat 13001 Kuwait; or PSC 1280 APO AE 09880-9000
telephone: [965] 2259-1001
FAX: [965] 2538-0282

Key Leaders:

Amir	SABAH al-Ahmad al-Jabir al-Sabah
Prime Min.	JABIR AL-MUBARAK al-Hamad al-Sabah
First Dep. Prime Min.	AHMAD al-Hamud al-Jabir al-Sabah
Dep. Prime Min.	AHMAD AL-KHALID al-Hamad al-Sabah
Dep. Prime Min.	SABAH AL-KHALID al-

	Hamad al-Sabah
Dep. Prime Min.	Mustafa al-Jassim al-SHAMALI
Dep. Prime Min. for Economic Affairs	
Dep. Prime Min. for Legal Affairs	Rashid abd al-Muhsin al-HAMMAD
Min. of Commerce & Industry	Anas al-Khalid al-SALIH
Min. of Communications	Salim al-UTHAYNA
Min. of Defense	AHMAD AL-KHALID al-Hamad al-Sabah
Min. of Education & Higher Education	Nayif Falah al-HAJ
Min. of Electricity & Water	Abdulaziz Abdulatif al-IBRAHIM
Min. of Finance	Mustafa al-Jassim al-SHAMALI
Min. of Foreign Affairs	SABAH AL-KHALID al-Hamad al-Sabah
Min. of Health	Muhammad Barak al-HAIFI
Min. of Information	SALMAN al-Sabah al-Sabah
Min. of Interior	AHMAD al-Hamud al-Jabir al-Sabah
Min. of Justice	Sharida al-MAUSHARJI

Min. of Oil	Hani Abd al-Aziz HUSAYN
Min. of Public Works	Abdulaziz Abdulatif al-IBRAHIM
Min. of Religious Endowment & Islamic Affairs	Sharida al-MAUSHARJI
Min. of Social Affairs & Labor	Thikra al-RASHIDI
Min. of State for Cabinet Affairs	MUHAMMAD Abdallah al-Mubarak al-Sabah
Min. of State for Development Affairs	Rawla DASHTI
Min. of State for Housing Affairs	Salim al-UTHAYNA
Min. of State for Municipal Affairs	MUHAMMAD Abdallah al-Mubarak al-Sabah
Min. of State for National Assembly Affairs	Rawla DASHTI
Governor, Central Bank of Kuwait	Muhammad al-HASHIL
Ambassador to the US	SALIM al-Abdallah al-Jabir al-Sabah
Permanent Representative to the UN, New York	Mansur Ayad al-UTAYBI

Flag description:

three equal horizontal bands of green (top), white, and red with a black trapezoid based on the hoist side; colors and design are based on the Arab Revolt flag of World War I; green represents fertile fields, white stands for purity, red denotes blood on Kuwaiti swords, black signifies the defeat of the enemy

National symbol(s):
golden falcon

National anthem:
name: "Al-Nasheed Al-Watani" (National Anthem)
lyrics/music: Ahmad MUSHARI al-Adwani/Ibrahim Nasir al-SOULA
note: adopted 1978; the anthem is only used on formal occasions

Chapter 5: Economy

Economy - overview:

Kuwait has a geographically small, but wealthy, relatively open economy with crude oil reserves of about 102 billion barrels - about 7% of world reserves. Petroleum accounts for nearly half of GDP, 95% of export revenues, and 95% of government income. Kuwaiti officials have committed to increasing oil production to 4 million barrels per day by 2020. The rise in global oil prices throughout 2011 and 2012 is reviving government consumption and economic growth. Kuwait has experienced a 20% increase in government budget revenue, which has led to higher budget expenditures, particularly wage hikes for many public sector employees. Kuwait has done little to diversify its economy, in part, because of this positive fiscal situation, and, in part, due to the poor business climate and the historically acrimonious relationship between the National Assembly and the executive branch, which has stymied most movement on economic reforms. In 2010, Kuwait passed an economic development plan that pledges to spend up to $130 billion over five years to diversify the economy away from oil, attract more investment, and boost private sector participation in the economy.

GDP (purchasing power parity):

$153.4 billion (2012 est.)

country comparison to the world: 62

$146 billion (2011 est.)

$137.4 billion (2010 est.)

note: data are in 2012 US dollars

GDP (official exchange rate):

$173.4 billion (2012 est.)

GDP - real growth rate:

5.1% (2012 est.)

country comparison to the world: 60

6.3% (2011 est.)

-2.4% (2010 est.)

GDP - per capita (PPP):

$40,500 (2012 est.)

country comparison to the world: 27

$39,700 (2011 est.)

$38,300 (2010 est.)

note: data are in 2012 US dollars

GDP - composition by sector:

agriculture: 0.3%

industry: 50.2%

services: 49.5% (2012 est.)

Labor force:

2.304 million

country comparison to the world: 116

note: non-Kuwaitis represent about 60% of the labor force (2012 est.)

Labor force - by occupation:

agriculture: NA%

industry: NA%

services: NA%

Unemployment rate:

2.2% (2004 est.)

country comparison to the world: 16

Population below poverty line:

NA%

Household income or consumption by percentage share:

lowest 10%: NA%

highest 10%: NA%

Investment (gross fixed):

14% of GDP (2012 est.)

country comparison to the world: 140

Budget:

revenues: $115.8 billion

expenditures: $58.08 billion (2012 est.)

Taxes and other revenues:

66.8% of GDP (2012 est.)

country comparison to the world: 5

Budget surplus (+) or deficit (-):

33.3% of GDP (2012 est.)

country comparison to the world: 1

Public debt:

6% of GDP (2012 est.)

country comparison to the world: 148

7.5% of GDP (2011 est.)

Inflation rate (consumer prices):

2.9% (2012 est.)

country comparison to the world: 89

4.7% (2011 est.)

Central bank discount rate:

1.25% (31 December 2010 est.)

country comparison to the world: 105

3% (31 December 2009 est.)

Commercial bank prime lending rate:

5% (31 December 2012 est.)

country comparison to the world: 156

5.2% (31 December 2011 est.)

Stock of narrow money:

$27.55 billion (31 December 2012 est.)

country comparison to the world: 61

$22.85 billion (31 December 2011 est.)

Stock of broad money:

$109.4 billion (31 December 2012 est.)

country comparison to the world: 52

$99.89 billion (31 December 2011 est.)

Stock of domestic credit:

$88.9 billion (31 December 2012 est.)

country comparison to the world: 54

$90.64 billion (31 December 2011 est.)

Market value of publicly traded shares:

$100.9 billion (31 December 2011)

country comparison to the world: 39

$119.6 billion (31 December 2010)

$95.94 billion (31 December 2009)

Agriculture - products:

fish

Industries:

petroleum, petrochemicals, cement, shipbuilding and repair, water desalination, food processing, construction materials

Industrial production growth rate:

10.2% (2012 est.)

country comparison to the world: 10

Current account balance:

$73.26 billion (2012 est.)

country comparison to the world: 8

$70.78 billion (2011 est.)

Exports:

$121 billion (2012 est.)

country comparison to the world: 35

$102.9 billion (2011 est.)

Exports - commodities:

oil and refined products, fertilizers

Exports - partners:

South Korea 16%, India 15.7%, Japan 13.4%, US 11.7%, China 9.2%, Singapore 4.2% (2012)

Imports:

$22.79 billion (2012 est.)

country comparison to the world: 74
$22.08 billion (2011 est.)

Imports - commodities:
food, construction materials, vehicles and parts, clothing

Imports - partners:
US 11.8%, China 9.2%, Saudi Arabia 8.3%, Japan 8.2%, South Korea 7%, Germany 5.1%, Italy 4.7%, India 4.6%, UAE 4.2% (2012)

Reserves of foreign exchange and gold:
$29 billion (31 December 2012 est.)
country comparison to the world: 52
$25.91 billion (31 December 2011 est.)

Debt - external:
$30.3 billion (31 December 2012 est.)
country comparison to the world: 72
$32.01 billion (31 December 2011 est.)

Stock of direct foreign investment - at home:
$4.645 billion (31 December 2012 est.)
country comparison to the world: 86
$2.768 billion (31 December 2011 est.)

Stock of direct foreign investment - abroad:
$56.07 billion (31 December 2012 est.)
country comparison to the world: 36
$48.4 billion (31 December 2011 est.)

Exchange rates:
Kuwaiti dinars (KD) per US dollar:
0.2799 (2012 est.)
0.276 (2011 est.)
0.2866 (2010 est.)
0.2877 (2009)
0.2679 (2008)

Fiscal year:

1 April - 31 March

Chapter 6: Energy

Electricity - production:
> 51.32 billion kWh (2010 est.)
> country comparison to the world: 51

Electricity - consumption:
> 43.41 billion kWh (2009 est.)
> country comparison to the world: 51

Electricity - exports:
> 0 kWh (2010 est.)
> country comparison to the world: 90

Electricity - imports:
> 0 kWh (2010 est.)
> country comparison to the world: 207

Electricity - installed generating capacity:
> 10.94 million kW (2009 est.)
> country comparison to the world: 52

Electricity - from fossil fuels:
> 100% of total installed capacity (2009 est.)
> country comparison to the world: 20

Electricity - from nuclear fuels:
> 0% of total installed capacity (2009 est.)
> country comparison to the world: 121

Electricity - from hydroelectric plants:
> 0% of total installed capacity (2009 est.)
> country comparison to the world: 178

Electricity - from other renewable sources:
> 0% of total installed capacity (2009 est.)
> country comparison to the world: 145

Crude oil - production:
> 2.682 million bbl/day (2011 est.)

country comparison to the world: 11

Crude oil - exports:

1.365 million bbl/day (2009 est.)

country comparison to the world: 11

Crude oil - imports:

0 bbl/day (2009 est.)

country comparison to the world: 204

Crude oil - proved reserves:

101.5 billion bbl (1 January 2013 est.)

country comparison to the world: 7

Refined petroleum products - production:

902,000 bbl/day (2008 est.)

country comparison to the world: 25

Refined petroleum products - consumption:

339,000 bbl/day (2011 est.)

country comparison to the world: 37

Refined petroleum products - exports:

717,700 bbl/day (2008 est.)

country comparison to the world: 10

Refined petroleum products - imports:

0 bbl/day (2008 est.)

country comparison to the world: 211

Natural gas - production:

11.73 billion cu m (2010 est.)

country comparison to the world: 42

Natural gas - consumption:

12.62 billion cu m (2010 est.)

country comparison to the world: 43

Natural gas - exports:

0 cu m (2010 est.)

country comparison to the world: 129

Natural gas - imports:
890 million cu m (2010 est.)
country comparison to the world: 60

Natural gas - proved reserves:
1.798 trillion cu m (1 January 2012 est.)
country comparison to the world: 21

Carbon dioxide emissions from consumption of energy:
81.33 million Mt (2010 est.)
country comparison to the world: 43

Chapter 7: Communications

Telephones - main lines in use:
514,700 (2011)
country comparison to the world: 98

Telephones - mobile cellular:
4.935 million (2011)
country comparison to the world: 105

Telephone system:
general assessment: the quality of service is excellent
domestic: new telephone exchanges provide a large capacity for new subscribers; trunk traffic is carried by microwave radio relay, coaxial cable, and open-wire and fiber-optic cable; a mobile-cellular telephone system operates throughout Kuwait, and the country is well supplied with pay telephones
international: country code - 965; linked to international submarine cable Fiber-Optic Link Around the Globe (FLAG); linked to Bahrain, Qatar, UAE via the Fiber-Optic Gulf (FOG) cable; coaxial cable and microwave radio relay to Saudi Arabia; satellite earth stations - 6 (3 Intelsat - 1 Atlantic Ocean and 2 Indian Ocean, 1 Inmarsat - Atlantic Ocean, and 2 Arabsat) (2011)

Broadcast media:
state-owned TV broadcaster operates 4 networks and a satellite channel; several private TV broadcasters have emerged since 2003; satellite TV available with pan-Arab TV stations especially popular; state-owned Radio Kuwait broadcasts on a number of channels in Arabic and English; first private radio station emerged in 2005; transmissions of at least 2 international radio broadcasters are available (2007)

Internet country code:
.kw

Internet hosts:
2,771 (2012)
country comparison to the world: 156

Internet users:

1.1 million (2009)
country comparison to the world: 96

Chapter 8: Transportation

Airports:

    7 (2012)

    country comparison to the world: 168

Airports - with paved runways:

    total: 4

    over 3,047 m: 1

    2,438 to 3,047 m: 2

    1,524 to 2,437 m: 1 (2012)

Airports - with unpaved runways:

    total: 3

    1,524 to 2,437 m: 1

    under 914 m: 2 (2012)

Heliports:

    4 (2012)

Pipelines:

    gas 261 km; oil 540 km; refined products 57 km (2013)

Roadways:

    total: 5,749 km

    country comparison to the world: 150

    paved: 4,887 km

    unpaved: 862 km (2004)

Merchant marine:

    total: 34

    country comparison to the world: 82

    by type: bulk carrier 2, carrier 3, container 6, liquefied gas 4, petroleum tanker 19

    registered in other countries: 45 (Bahamas 1, Bahrain 5, Comoros 1, Libya 1, Malta 3, Marshall Islands 2, Panama 12, Qatar 6, Saudi Arabia 4, UAE 10) (2010)

Ports and terminals:

Ash Shu'aybah, Ash Shuwaykh, Az Zawr (Mina' Sa'ud), Mina' 'Abd Allah, Mina' al Ahmadi

Chapter 9: Military

Military branches:

Kuwaiti Land Forces (KLF), Kuwaiti Navy, Kuwaiti Air Force (Al-Quwwat al-Jawwiya al-Kuwaitiya; includes Kuwaiti Air Defense Force, KADF), Kuwaiti National Guard (KNG) (2013)

Military service age and obligation:

17-21 years of age for voluntary military service; conscription suspended (2012)

Manpower available for military service:

males age 16-49: 1,002,480

females age 16-49: 616,958 (2010 est.)

Manpower fit for military service:

males age 16-49: 840,912

females age 16-49: 523,206 (2010 est.)

Manpower reaching militarily significant age annually:

male: 17,653

female: 16,232 (2010 est.)

Military expenditures:

3.7% of GDP (2012)

country comparison to the world: 28

Chapter 10: Transnational Issues

Disputes - international:
   Kuwait and Saudi Arabia continue negotiating a joint maritime boundary with Iran; no maritime boundary exists with Iraq in the Persian Gulf

Trafficking in persons:
   current situation: Kuwait is a destination country for men and women subjected to forced labor and, to a lesser degree, forced prostitution; men and women migrate from India, Egypt, Bangladesh, Syria, Pakistan, the Philippines, Sri Lanka, Indonesia, Nepal, Iran, Jordan, Ethiopia, and Iraq to work in Kuwait, most of them in the domestic service, construction, and sanitation sectors; although most of these migrants enter Kuwait voluntarily, upon arrival some are subjected to conditions of forced labor by their sponsors and labor agents, including nonpayment of wages, long working hours without rest, deprivation of food, threats, physical or sexual abuse, and restrictions on movement, such as the withholding of passports or confinement to the workplace

   tier rating: Tier 3 - Kuwait does not fully comply with the minimum standards for the elimination of trafficking and is not making sufficient efforts to do so; the government did not enact its draft comprehensive anti-trafficking law; Kuwait's victim-protection measures remain weak, particularly due to its lack of proactive victim-identification procedures and continued reliance on the sponsorship system, which causes victims of trafficking to be punished for immigration violations rather than protected (2009)

Map of Kuwait

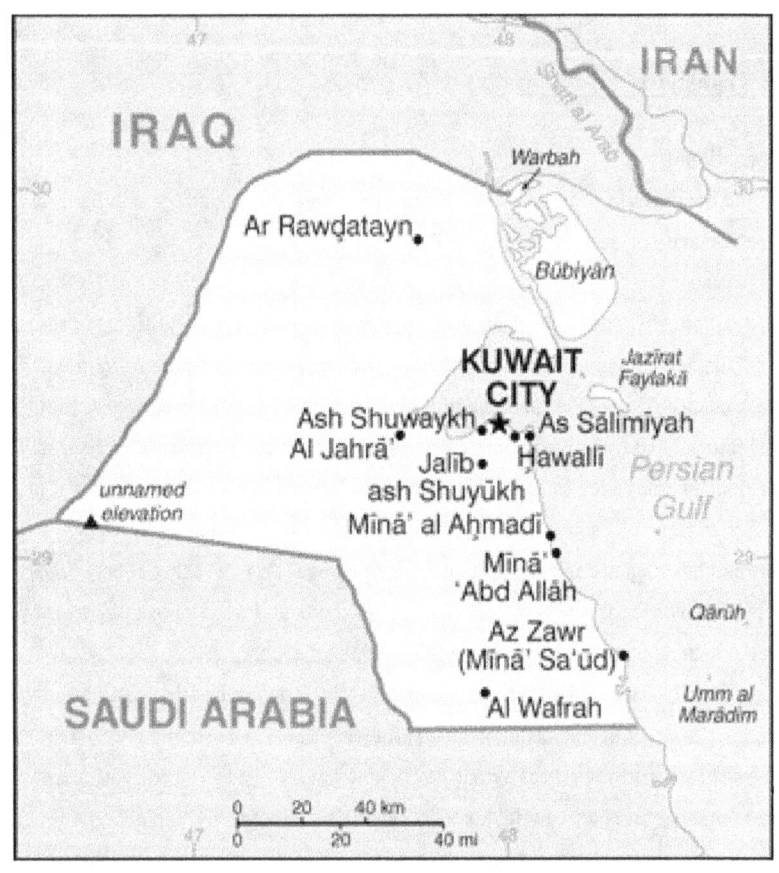

Other Key Facts™ Titles

Key Facts on Syria

Key Facts on China

Key Facts on Qatar

Key Facts on India

Key Facts on Germany

Key Facts on Argentina

Key Facts on Russia

Key Facts on North Korea

Key Facts on Brazil

Key Facts on Italy

Key Facts on the United Arab Emirates

Key Facts on the European Union

Key Facts on Pakistan

Key Facts on Saudi Arabia

Key Facts on Cyprus

Key Facts on Iran

Key Facts on Afghanistan

Key Facts on Iraq

Key Facts on Indonesia

Key Facts on South Korea

Key Facts on France

Key Facts on the United Kingdom

Key Facts on Egypt

Key Facts on Israel

Key Facts on Mexico

Key Facts on the United States of America
Key Facts on Turkey
Key Facts on South Africa
Key Facts on Greece
Key Facts on Japan
Key Facts on Malaysia
Key Facts on Vietnam
Key Facts on Hong Kong
Key Facts on Jordan
Key Facts on Australia
Key Facts on Venezuela
Key Facts on Canada
Key Facts on Burma (Myanmar)
Key Facts on Myanmar (Burma)
Key Facts on Singapore
Key Facts on Ireland
Key Facts on The Philippines
Key Facts on Thailand
Key Facts on Yemen
Key Facts on Bahrain
All Key Facts™ Titles are Available at www.Amazon.com

THE INTERNATIONALIST®
2013
WWW.INTERNATIONALIST.COM

www.ingramcontent.com/pod-product-compliance
Lightning Source LLC
Chambersburg PA
CBHW070728180526
45167CB00004B/1661